whichever music

poetry

kate potts

tall-lighthouse

Acknowledgements: Thanks to the editors of *Magma* and
The Wolf, where some of these poems, or versions of the
poems first appeared.

Thanks to Roddy Lumsden, James Byrne, The Wolf Workshop
participants (summer 2007), and the various members of the ex-
Goldsmiths Wednesday workshop, for their support and advice.

Thanks also to Michael Fernando, Holly Bembridge, David
Downing, and The Family.

cover image : mat redvers

cover photo : will strange

© Kate Potts 2008
Kate Potts has asserted her right under
the Copyright, Design and Patents Act 1988
to be identified as the author of this work.

tall-lighthouse pilot publication - new poetry
from young poets - series edited by Roddy Lumsden
and supported by Arts Council England

ISBN 978-1-904551- 51-5
tall-lighthouse
www.tall-lighthouse.co.uk

contents

Ghost no. 1	1
Ghost no. 2	2
Homemaking	3
Proof, Maybe	4
Life in Space	5
Subject	6
Acrobat Falls	7
Magpie	8
Flashpoint	9
A Partridge – A Pear Tree	10
The end of civilisation	11
Flit	12
Insomnia Chant	13
Galatea/ *Pygmalion*, Sunday morning	14
The Learning	15
Compendium of Water	16
Tread, Softly	17

*Imperceptibly the love of those discords grew
upon me as my love of music grew stronger.*
Edgar Allen Poe

Ghost no. 1

Phantom heels stalk the corridor:
click, click. My watery iris
at the fisheye. You are an amalgam
of angles, crystalline in denim.

I snap supermarket bags at your ears,
shuffle crockery, mimic the telephone
with the chirp at the tips of my teeth.
I'm a conjurer of uneasiness, spectre

of barely remembered door keys,
gas hob, medicine, disconsolate
child – your crush of vodka'd limbs.
Mine's the suspension of breath.

You contemplate chaos, prostration,
beginning again in a new place
under a new name. I am the ice
in your liver – exhaled.

Ghost no. 2

Homeward, the concrete's all velour,
a back-lit backdrop to your tapdance.
Nobody's watching. The sun's still
subterranean, haloing sleeping brick.

You tightrope walk the cracks, sense
bug-curled bodies fluttering in beds
or smoking cigarettes determinedly
on balconies – their minute, orange pulses.

There's an understated warmth
of sound: refrigerators, lightbulbs,
hidden spectra mumbling. At this hour
the city is palpable, freshly printed.

We lunge at the lightening edges,
shake the pattern out and hug the page
around our waning limbs, bassnote
wingbeats echoing our blood.

Homemaking

The heavy, moulded wood of their lives
glows lustrous, purrs as she polishes.
In photos they're invincible, the English –

limbs wound tight on baize lawns.
It's always the same half-cocked smile
as if to a mother. Her mouth

is not her own, creases in sympathy.
The rooms are dense with their smell,
sweet, as if under glass, and somewhere

there's the vinegar kick of putrescence,
fruit just blossoming, falling into itself
beneath the oven, behind the skirting boards.

She lifts the receiver, dials Grandpa's
Warsaw flat – eighth floor, silty block
on the link road. *Jak się masz?*

His voice is liquor velvet, content
in container trucks' rolling bass, the soft pat
of jittery fingers. He doesn't hear so well,

but guesses, probably, with a squint at the wire,
the unspoken demands. *Oczywiście!*
The telephone sprawls – her strained ear –

relays a rattling of coffee mugs,
blaring repeats of *Columbo*. She remembers
the photographs there. Pinned, unframed,

demurely curling. The faces are blasted free
of colour and heads and feet are lopped
but the shutter has cradled them all.

They've trusted its aluminium *clack*
to harden the instant.
Light in their eyes, jutted chins.

Proof, Maybe

The light's buttercups – quick, mossed water.
Mister, behind the lens layer, scopes her:
grand, fly-goggle glasses and cribbed grin,
dog lead slung loose around her neck.

We daughters – her ducks – putter behind,
lagging, diminishing in height.
We girls, armed with buckets, shrimp-nets,
and our own, more brittle cameras.

His one, gigantic eye dilates, tightens –
pure cornea – calculated focus and aperture,
a question of degrees.

We took the girls out to Westerham. It was August.
Swish car, upholstery, house in the city,
a dopping of learning about your name – *Doctor* –
remember that phone book call in the early hours,
the man whose wife was giving birth?

We are squinting in gingham, growing, intractable.
Not insomnia's spite, cussed day, kicked teeth
but an accumulation of glossy paper,
irrefutable fact, brisk walks.

Kafka had a sign over his desk that read, simply, WAIT.
Words seize – bleach – are not enough.

Life in Space

*Coming back to earth was a very sad time for me
– partly because I just didn't want to come back just then.*
                                    Helen Sharman

Wait there says Sir, face mottled and blooming,
that sing-song edge to his burr.
And he's lost. Sliced in a surge of carriages,
harried suits. We know – one clotted, stalling herd –
we'll be too late to see the first Briton in space.

We vision her: pickled, part-weightless,
charged, secreting the luminous shock –
a brackish, tender, blue-green earth,
diminutive beside her splayed hands.

Probably not like us – our worn perimeter
of Norwood Streets, chips on the homeward loiter.
Leery, at the station's edge, we practice
the glint of dagger eyes, our noxious *tut*

but in such commuterland we're close
to subsidence, a puddle of spiderish,
laddered tights, our cardigans pulled, bulbous
at the sleeves. We hoist our bodies up. Breathe.

Subject

> *Our "subjects" procured in those days under*
> *difficulties, & at great expense (often smuggled)*
> *proved curiously instructive in pathology too.*

We're darers, Michael and I, cadged keys and gathered
steel. They seep formaldehyde

at the hairlines – those glutinous fruit, spools of fibre
and pulp in glass keepers.

They crow gristle – aspic sets of bladder, spleen, skin
pillowed in fat, frontal lobes

shrunken cumulonimbus – the space, in layers:
furniture stacks, carpet-must

and cast iron, tiered galleries; the skulls, ink-mapped
into hemispheres, forked subsets:

negro, aborigine. A womb-slice nestles the foetus –
cartoon fingers, milkish. Asleep –

clean perfection – the child she bellied in hunger,
in pluck, still, holding out for the war's end.

Acrobat Falls

Atrophied flight:
from star-armed hushing of ripe air
to a chin bone crump, grit in the gums,
between your soft teeth.

*

The night's conversation:
you hoick at a word. The map slips –
whole, oily continents spinning
through faultlines: fizzing, delicious.

*

A breathless crumble and thud.
His goodbye fingers a tiny, unnamed bone
that undoes, howls you
out into the highroad's glass wind.

Magpie

I grasp my spoils with yellow knuckles,
hoard reflections, bask in silver.

There are fifty seven pieces in my boot box,
all of them fingered and loved to sore brightness:

this feather-spun choker's a gift, sneaked
from a pocket to save the intended, this anklet's bells

tsk at the smallest movement, lullaby me
when silence threatens. The charm bracelet

belonged to his mother. Most are scavenged.
I've a nose for the scent of silver.

It's the oily calm of the winter Thames, an edge
like the tartness of gin. I like to imagine

my blood's a thread of wrought sterling.
Without these charms I'm animal, tender.

Flashpoint

Memory won't let you flinch.
Each baroque facade's a frame on a screel.
You swing a left at the temporary lights
then stall by the railway bridge, confused –

someone has flipped the diversion signs.
You're fixing closer in on a loop.
Here is a girl in your own rare skin,
grocery bags held to her chest like dumbbells

and here is a house: four windows,
though slug trails silver the paisley.
Here are the haiku:
spent magic, honking dodos, puttering gently.

The cellar's scrawled with Wicca runes.
Intestinal pipes and wires mewl,
hollow in the fug. Here's a bathful
of acrid wine from a chemical kit.

The sink hiccups ash – you spit, then gulp
at the tap. Observe the morning's sallow distance,
flattening time to a promise, rooms to stills.
Their bodies are flesh-swaddled bones

coddled in mattress shallows and pits.
She breathes this – his placid bulk, their sweat –
and curls herself deeper into what's left of the dark,
bracing them both against the blast.

A Partridge – A Pear Tree

The first day: Truelove sends
a shushed blue morning hour, the mute
absurdity of tarmac, a sobering of worn toes –
the upbeat's echo dredges us home.

Second, he sends books, and underlinings –
Sartre's mutter – something is beginning.
The words stem: flesh-nub,
furling bruise of a clear, new shoot.

We cultivate with iron tea and hours:
milk swigs, sweet drams, the open breath
of television at the schedule's finish,
lush with nebula and static,

Johnny's tender, breakfast croon.
The fruits set, wax, fluid and flesh,
specked skin – a fatty, nibbled velvet.
At four a.m. he cawls,

true as a child's crayoned circle of bird –
twig-foot, shut-eye. He's
no hart, nor dove, but gamey,
winter market plume.

His is a glistering, brass whirr
of wings, a glide – a chestnut tail.
I put by the feathers;
ease the meat from the bone.

The end of civilisation

I slip my sandals off and skim
the taut skin of his ankle beneath the table.
The cloth hangs in heavy, pristine folds.

He has tasted the plummy wine.
The glasses are poised on exquisite,
snappable stalks. My hands unknit –

I chance an elbow, risk a glance, shot
over my shoulder. Will we pass?
He's clammy, marble-fingered, but,

from a distance, convincing.
It is more a chuckle than a howl. I order
the cheapest dish and consider my bouquet:

a spindly, top-heavy bundle
of full-blown tulips. His teeth grind, softly,
the coda of each measured flurry of words.

I lift my chin and straighten, ratchet
the corners of my mouth and eyes –
that familiar warmth – entranced

by the others, their regular dance,
the tussle of cutlery. I want to remove
this pall-cloth – one, neat flick

of the wrist, see! Only just flecked
with the smirch of gravy and wine, the slaver
of porcelain on plaster, and,

while they're distracted, flit us to the park
with a paper bag of fat, crumpling chips
to witness the slow smear of dusk.

Flit

Like a Wednesday matinee film, this leaving, a last
slow burn and a skip out, his sly mouth drawn thin.
Your new-cooled eyes survey the walls, the plaster
fractures, blue dust laid in pelts. You're loose,

skinned – a stark brew – prodding the bag of leaves
as if it holds last tannin, last tea-kick – strong
as a horse – husked chords on the phone to the office.
You're not yourself. You're someone ductile, burnished.

You – thick-lipsticked, filling a canvas bag with apples,
the end of a loaf. The chemist hawks lotion, sunglasses,
bleach. You – minnowing up the baked streets,
sharper, each tread slicing August clean open. You –

sleek purpose, stalled on the station concourse,
mouthing the litany of departures, prising the coast
and spitting the rest of the fruit. Then headed out,
hitched to the engine's momentum, lighter

as the land falls. You – picture postcard – skirting
the main street, kicking at dune-shins, wallowing
                                                                further,
treading water. The cowl of your new-shed skin's
a cool star, a map point away on the shingle,

cupped in the tideline's tar and trash. You – hours on –
salted, dried, and sewn back in, hugging the hook
of your knees, gums a swill of vinegared chips and
                                                                wine –
the pip and blurt of the arcades hauling you in, slowing,

loping back to the town's eyes, train's cradle.
Concourse. Clay city-streets. Stupefied bed.

Insomnia Chant

No such greasy twist of sheets, spun, fettering sleep's
drop. No plastered wall, pod, stiff cell.

This city's a winked fractal, wheeled in dark. I skulk
to the near cool of the disused railway

spun in bramble and bind-weed, gnat-shored, banked
in mud. I'll envision no sheep, no floss of beach surf

welled on sand. No apposite mending of other bodies,
patching of loss, rents, frowns, in brown paper,

goodwill and duct tape. No making right, no making,
no yield – lovers' backward curses germing

in my glands. No configuring of scale, paucity, those
others – their night hands, tranced, shuffling

memory aces – that time we woke. Same instant. Four –
his mother sleeping in the next room, flourine

eyes in the closed dark. No wheedling after sense, home,
what was sold. No drawing under no river. No

hands, gentler. Soft-snared comma, spun, spore-lit
spiral nothing, hauling radiation, matter – gone.

Galatea/ *Pygmalion*, Sunday morning

Ignite at the eye's cool centre, haul the onioned iris
wider – wormhole gnawing at blue – tight witness.

Avoid the look of the eyes – pale meat –
grit oysters – spit-swabbed.

Your mind clump's February's pudding, hinged
like tinny umbilical, twisting. Worry it.

There's a hint – peat gone-ness of intestine
but she's cauterised, more stone than skin.

Worry the names: mattress warp, soft eel of stunned
body – hot consonants radioed in to new maps.

She'll outlast you – modelled as if set to spring,
twitching now – vigilant temples, lashes –

Broadcast the nerve. Branch current through
methylate tissue. Hang to the ion, pulse,

though mimicking litheness can be
puppetry – seized string –

shake smoke, draggle sleep –
scoop the cuttered, yellow-tree morning

and drink the exposure, the flush
configuration – his features, face.

The Learning

Bee-drip of the learning, I mouth my country –
this Shakespeare fast-food multi tug.
They leave the compounds at night, tell
no-one, taxi down, the early morning cattle

little painted engines, stalled in lots. Always,
it rains. We sidle, best fit the adjectives,
the idiom. If you are first to be punched, then
there's time to rub it better. This boy tells

Kipling, 'My Last Duchess,' Welfare State.
We spell inventories of home, exactitudes:
bed, folded stool, TV, Kabul – thin summoning.
The classroom's a graveyard; this girl wants

to dance at my wedding. Half of it's spy rules –
when to slang and not, the variegated tongue,
the laws of interview, of application; never
enough space, hours, quality, or value.

We spell Igbo and Urhobo, alekum asalaam.
They like, and do not like this Shakespeare –
this, the history: *My father was proud.*
Like a true king, at my birth I did not cry.

Compendium of Water

- Roof-leak, drench for beached fins, first and last thing – branded, filched glassfuls.

- Litre jugs drunk pig-cheeked, barefoot, poured and lain in, pruning skin to mush, feet to webbing slaps.

- Chiming pints, bedside and bath edge, crusted, condensing, sweet as ulcer and gum.

- Possibility nurtured by hills, that last scarp, premonition of slug's trail sea.

- Pipes bark, trundle – the whale-cry of solitary, braking buses.

- Insomnia chant for a child slipping, flat-footed, as if over snow, down to the kitchen's lowing, sink –

- this hankered spool of light, transmuted, tap to tongue.

Tread, Softly

Carriage winds graze cheeks. Mice gnaw steel.
Your body's lightwaves, dreamstuff,
eyes fixed to the tunnel's fissures, glossies

of skin, Nintendo, caffeine pills. Reconstitute
and your world shudders to halt, each frame
a shock. You nod, nuzzle newsprint dailies,

scan the shoe parade, molar-cream paint, wait –
pick at clavicle, knuckle, snort the Minotaur's
drizzle and wheeze, the scads of stuttered bone,

the beauty: all our bleary flesh, like sniffs
of new, raw milk. We're a sappy litter
fantasising morning, each one's eye turned in

to pearl, to mirroring. Pinch shut your lids
and shuffle the day: nested bedsheets, bath iron,
spattered ash of coffee, downed, as medicine.

They're such little, petulant gods that nail
our wants: lacquered dirt, part
remembered – all adulterated earth

and all need's for your own flesh
warmed up in his – and all their voices –
any voice – whichever music.